Penguin Modern Poets

7

RICHARD MURPHY

JON SILKIN

NATHANIEL TARN

Penguin Books

Penguin Books Ltd, Harmondsworth, Middlesex, England
Penguin Books Australia Ltd, Ringwood, Victoria, Australia

—

This selection first published 1965
Reprinted 1968, 1970

—

—

Made and printed in Great Britain
by Cox & Wyman Ltd,
London, Reading and Fakenham
Set in Monotype Garamond

Contents

NATHANIEL TARN

ACKNOWLEDGEMENTS

The poems in this selection are taken from the following books, to whose publishers acknowledgement is made: *Sailing to an Island* (1963), by Richard Murphy, published by Faber & Faber; *The Peaceable Kingdom* (1954), *The Re-ordering of the Stones* (1961), and *Nature with Man* (1965), by Jon Silkin, published by Chatto and Windus; *Old Savage/Young City* (1964), by Nathaniel Tarn, published by Jonathan Cape. Certain new poems have appeared in the *Listener*, *The Times Literary Supplement*, the *Spectator*, *Stand*, *Peacock*, *Ambit*, and *Agenda*.

RICHARD MURPHY

The Cleggan Disaster

OFF THE WEST COAST OF IRELAND IN 1927

Five boats were shooting their nets in the bay
After dark. It was cold and late October.
The hulls hissed and rolled on the sea's black hearth
In the shadow of stacks close to the island.
Rain drenched the rowers, with no drying wind.
From the strokes of the oars a green fire flaked
And briskly quenched. The shore-lights were markers
Easterly shining across the Blind Sound.

Five pieces of drift-net with a mesh of diamonds
Were paid from each stern. The webbed curtains hung
Straight from the cork-lines, and warps were hitched
To the strong stems, and the pine oars boarded.
The men in the boats drew their pipes and rested.

The tide fell slack, all the breakers were still.
Not a flicker of a fish, only the slow fall
Of the ocean there drawing out the last drops of sleep.
Soon they could feel the effort of the ebb
Yearning at the yarn, twitching their mooring-stones
Stealthily seawards. Two boats began to haul.

From the bows of a boat in the centre of the bay
Concannon watched and waited. On each far wing
He heard them hauling. He held in his hand
The strong hemp rope which stretched from the cork-line
So that his fingers could feel the cord throb
If the shoal struck the nets. But so far, nothing.

Why had those others hauled? They were old
And experienced boatsmen. One man on the quay
At Bofin warned him, 'Sharpen your knife,

Be ready for trouble, cut away your nets.
Your crew is too young.' Were they going home?
Would the night not remain calm enough to fill
The barrels in their barns with food for the winter?

He had respect for the sea. He gave away
A share of his catch at the Cleggan market.
No one who asked for a feed of fish was refused.
On Bofin island, he loafed on land,
Dozed the sterile winter dreaming of boats,
But in summer wanted neither food nor sleep
While he gave his strength seriously to the sea.

He was sure of his boat, though small, well built.
Her ribs and her keel were adzed out of oak,
Her thole-pins were cut out of green holly,
And the grapnel was forged by the Cleggan smith.
Since the day she was launched, she had been lucky.

He was doubtful of his crew: three men and a boy
Who needed the money. Their land was poor,
But they had no heart for this work on water.
They helped each other. There were throngs of children
In thatched houses, whose lights they could see
Sparkling on the island, dim specks at Cleggan.
That night the best of boatsmen were on the bay
And many who wished they had waited by the fire.

In the dark before the moon rose, driftingly he smelt
Faintly on the water a floating oil
Bleeding from the nets where a blue-shark havocked
On the quivering tails of a mackerel shoal.
So he hauled until he reached the snarled threshes
Of the snapping shark, which he stunned across the rail
And clubbed with a foot-stick, bursting its blood.

Iron shouts clanged round the horse-shoe bay
From the fetlock gap to the broad channel
As luck began to load the farthest nets,
And the green mackerel river raced through the water,
Crossed over the gunwales, and jetted fire
In the black braziers of the rolling bilges.

He thought, as the lucky stream continued to flow,
'There are three more pieces of net to be hauled.
If we're too greedy, we could sink the boat.
We have enough now to row home safely.
Cut them in time and return in the daylight.
Darker it's getting, with a north-west wind.'

The night was like a shell, with long sea surges
Loudening from afar, though no one was listening.
Quickly they folded the nets and heaped the fish.
The moon was kindling. The sky smouldered like soot.
Warm gusts of air floated by, moist with dew.
Mackerel flapped in the bilges. A woman was calling,
Crying from the beach. A shiver rippled the spine
Of the stony headland. Then, on the glistening gong
Of the sleeping sea, terrible hailstones hammered.

A storm began to march, the shrill wind piping
And thunder exploding, while the lightning flaked
In willow cascades, and the bayonets of hail
Flashed over craters and hillocks of water.
All the boats were trapped. None had reached the pier.
The target of the gale was the mainland rocks.

The men began to pray. The stack-funnelled hail
Crackled in volleys, with blasts on the bows
Where Concannon stood to fend with his body
The slash of seas. Then sickness surged,
And against their will they were griped with terror.

He told them to bail. When they lost the bailer
They bailed with their boots. Then they cast overboard
Their costly nets and a thousand mackerel.

She was drifting down the sound, her mooring-stone lifted
By the fingers of the tide plucking at the nets
Which he held with scorching hands. Over and over
He heard in his heart, 'Keep her stem to the storm,
And the nets will help her to ride the water;
Meet the force of the seas with her bows,
Each wave as it comes.' He'd use the knife later.

Down in the deep where the storm could not go
The ebb-tide, massive and slow, was drawing
Windwards the ninety-six fathom of nets
With hundreds of mackerel thickly meshed,
Safely tugging the boat off the mainland shore.
The moon couldn't shine, the clouds shut her out,
But she came unseen to sway on his side
All the waters gathered from the great spring tide.

As he slid from the cliff-slope of a heaped wave
Down the white and violet skin of turbulence
Into the boiling trough, he gathered in
Loose hanks of net, until the scalding rope
Steamed from his hands, the brittle boat, convulsed
By the far crest, shot through the spindrift safe.

The oarsmen were calling Concannon to let go,
Take it easy for a while. Let the boat drift
To the Cleggan shore, down wind, till they touch land.
Even there, if they died, it would be in a bay
Fringed with friends' houses, instead of in the open
Ocean, where the lost would never be found,
Where nothing is buried, no prayers are said.
Concannon silenced them, and stiffened his hold.

Twice the lightning blinked, then a crash of thunder.
Three cliffs of waves collapsed above them, seas
Crushed in his face, he fell down, and was dazed.

The wind began to play, like country fiddlers
In a crowded room, with nailed boots stamping
On the stone cottage floor, raising white ashes.
The sea became a dance. He staggered to the floor
As the music unleashed him, spun in a circle.
Now he was dancing round the siege of Death:
Now he was Death, they were dancing around him,
White robed dancers with crowns and clubs,
With white masked faces, and hands like claws
Flaying his eyes, as they clinched and swung.
He was holding the rope as the dance subsided.

While he lay there stunned, he remembered the sea
In the tar-melting sunlight, dry weed on the thwarts,
The gills of mackerel tight in the meshes,
Hot stench of dead fish in the bailer,
And the planks gaping wide, and the thole-pins screeching,
The lines like lathes grooving the gunwales
While the depths yielded up the sacred John Dory.
He would never say, like that cripple on the quay,
He wished he had not wasted his life on the sea.

He knelt against the stem, his hands bleeding,
His eyes, scalded by the scurf of salt,
Straining to give shape to the shadows they saw
That looked like men in the milder water.
One of the crew said he heard his brother
Shouting for help, two oars away,
Yet when he hollowed, there was no reply.
In a lightning flash, a white hand rose
And rested on the gunwale, then slowly sank.

Down the valleys of this lull, like a black cow
In search of her calf, an upturned hull
Wallowed towards them. Her stem had parted.
All hands must have been lost. She lunged to his side
And almost staved him. Were the men inside?
Those who had thrown him his ropes from the quay?
The one who had warned him about his crew?
No help for them now. With his foot on her planks
He fended her off. As she bore away,
Her keel like a scythe cut a clear white swath
Through the gale's acres. Then a great sea crossed.

On the far side, as he nipped among white horses
Bolting towards him, under the streamers of manes
And the quick hoof-lash, he still headed the storm:
The chargers' lances hurtled with little harm
Through the icy air, while their hooves plunged on.

Now, though sea-boils encrusted his eyes,
He saw the Lyon Light, in spurts when they rode
Upon grey shoulders, flicker from white to red.
Lumps of water licked across tidal shallows.
They cantered at walls, and then faced hills.
The horses stampeded, as lanes closed ahead
In a white chalk-cliff. Rolled under horses
With manes in their mouths, their bones smashed,
Their blood washed away. . . . Yet the cliff was passing.
The water rose to the thwarts. They went on bailing.

What were those lights that seemed to blaze like red
Fires in the pits of waves, lifted and hurled
At the aching sockets of his eyes, coals that lit
And expired in the space of a swell's slow heave?
'Am I going blind? *Am I going blind?*' he thought.
'Look at that wave. How it sharpens into a rock.

WATCH THAT ROCK. GET READY TO JUMP. It's gone.
Now *there's* a light . . . count the seconds: a slow pulse.
I can see that light from my own back door,
Slyne Head, never so high, such piercing brightness.
Where has it gone? Spears in hundreds are hurtling
Against my head. Was it south of us it shone?
Lucky the keepers are safe. What a lonely life.
The lamps on the headlands have all been snuffed
By smothering waves. What weak pulse in the stars.
If I knew how to read them, we were saved.'

Lights flickered and vanished. Like a grey seal
Blinded by shot, he clung to the stem, his eyes closed.
The boy whispered. 'There's rocks to leeward.'
'What rocks do you think?' another asked.
'Dog Rock, I think, I fished here last summer.'
Concannon opened his knife: 'I'm cutting the nets.'
Piece by piece he slashed, but he had to tear
The clinging hanks with his finger bones, at last
He severed the rope, their guide on that dire sea-road,
And sank to his knees. The boatsmen rowed,
Backwards, falling away, her stem still to the storm,
With their eyes fixed on the faint lamps
That led across calm waters to Cleggan Quay.

It was three o'clock when she nudged the steps.
Safe on the stone bollards they fastened their ropes.
The full moon was whitening the ribs of hulks
In the worm-dark dock. The tide was flowing
As they trudged to the village. His crew helped him:
The sea had not claimed him, she had left him blind.

Lanterns shafted from the gates of the fish-store
Freshly that night cleaned for a *ceili*.*
Bodies of fishermen lay on the floor on boxes,

* *Ceili* (Irish) pronounced 'kayly' means 'a dance'.

Blood on their faces. Five had been found
By troops of searchers on shingle and sand.
Over the bier, with one hand cupping a flame,
An old man was looking at his drowned son.

As the day dawned, gap after gap was filled.
One of the boats was found on the beach at Letter
And floated off on the morning tide.
Only one body was got, the skull fractured:
Above high-water mark he had crawled and died.
The walking-stick of a man who was lame
Was thrown in a heap of rods on a silver strand.
There was a king of the Mayo fishermen
Drawn from the sea in the chain of his own nets.
Of those who survived, a young one was seen
Walking at noon in the fields, clutching a bailer.

A sleep, cordoned by memories, calmed the sea.
Dead bracken was rusting the headlands,
The hills were flaked with hoarfrost, the sky marbled
Like mackerel netted in June water
When they pulled the long oars for their island home.
Concannon's eyes were dark, like smithy troughs
Where hot harpoons are plunged, they boiled with pain.
Blindly he rowed, facing the hidden sun.

They passed the tower in the harbour's mouth
Snow-white on the gun-rock, the two round towers
Touching each other on green fields, the castle
Of Cromwell's crimes full of screeching choughs.
Women in shawls on the quay were waiting.

The funeral boats brought over the bodies found,
But most were carried away on the great ebb-tide.
From the village of Rossadillisk they lost sixteen
And from Bofin nine. One man above all was blind.

In a common grave that was dug in the sand-dunes
Close to high-water mark but leagues from low springs
They laid side by side the deal-board coffins
Lowering them on ropes, then shovelled the fine sand
Which whisperingly slid round their recent companions,
And sometimes the shovels met with a knelling clang
While in shifts they worked till the mound was raised.

After the prayers were said and the graveyard closed
Concannon was counting the fifty steps to his house,
Working out sounds, the sea-fall on the beach.
Would the islanders ever again dare to fish?
When he'd mastered this dark road, he himself would ask
To be oarsman in a boat, and mend the nets on land.
The croak of a herring-gull tolled across the sky.
An oyster-catcher squealed. Shoals broke on the bay.
The flood-tide rose and covered the deserted strand.

(*Years Later*)

Whose is that hulk on the shingle
The boatwright's son repairs
Though she has not been fishing
For thirty-four years
Since she rode the disaster?
The oars were turned into rafters
For a roof stripped by a gale.
Moss has grown on her keel.

Where are the red-haired women
Chattering along the piers
Who gutted millions of mackerel
And baited the spillet hooks
With mussels and lug-worms?
All the hurtful hours

Thinking the boats were coming
They hold against those years.

Where are the barefoot children
With brown toes in the ashes
Who went to the well for water,
Picked winkles on the beach
And gathered sea-rods in winter?
The lime is green on the stone
Which they once kept white-washed.
In summer nettles return.

Where are the dances in houses
With porter and cakes in the room,
The reddled faces of fiddlers
Sawing out jigs and reels,
The flickering eyes of neighbours?
The thatch which was neatly bordered
By a fringe of sea-stones
Has now caved in.

Why does she stand at the curtains
Combing her seal-grey hair
And uttering bitter opinions
On land-work and sea-fear,
Drownings and famines?
When will her son say,
'Forget about the disaster,
We're mounting nets today!'

Epitaph on a Fir-Tree

She grew ninety years through sombre winter,
Rhododendron summer of midges and rain,
In a beechwood scarred by the auctioneer,

Till a March evening, the garden work done,
It seemed her long life had been completed,
No further growth, no gaiety could remain.

At a wedding breakfast bridesmaids planted
With trowel and gloves this imported fir.
How soon, measured by trees, the party ended.

Arbour and crinoline have gone under
The laurel, gazebos under the yews:
Wood for wood, we have little to compare.

We think no more of granite steps and pews,
Or an officer patched with a crude trepan
Who fought in Rangoon for these quiet acres.

Axes and saws now convert the evergreen
Imperial shadows into deal boards,
And let the sun enter our house again.

Quickly we'll spend the rings that she hoarded
In her gross girth. The evening is ours.
Those delicate girls who earthed her up are faded.

Except for daffodils, the ground is bare:
We two are left. They walked through pergolas
And planted well, so that we might do better.

The Philosopher and the Birds

IN MEMORY OF WITTGENSTEIN AT ROSROE

A solitary invalid in a fuchsia garden
Where time's rain eroded the root since Eden,
He became for a tenebrous epoch the stone.

Here wisdom surrendered the don's gown
Choosing, for Cambridge, two deck chairs,
A kitchen table, undiluted sun.

He clipped with February shears the dead
Metaphysical foliage. Old, in fieldfares
Fantasies rebelled though annihilated.

He was haunted by gulls beyond omega shade,
His nerve tormented by terrified knots
In pin-feathered flesh. But all folly repeats

Is worth one snared robin his fingers untied.
He broke prisons, beginning with words,
And at last tamed, by talking, wild birds.

Through accident of place, now by belief
I follow his love which bird-handled thoughts
To grasp growth's terror or death's leaf.

He last on this savage promontory shored
His logical weapon. Genius stirred
A soaring intolerance to teach a blackbird.

So before alpha you may still hear sing
In the leaf-dark dusk some descended young
Who exalt the evening to a wordless song.

His wisdom widens: he becomes worlds
Where thoughts are wings. But at Rosroe hordes
Of village cats have massacred his birds.

The Poet on the Island

TO THEODORE ROETHKE

On a wet night, laden with books for luggage,
And stumbling under the burden of himself,
He reached the pier, looking for a refuge.

Darkly he crossed to the island six miles off:
The engine pulsed, the sails invented rhythm,
While the sea expanded and the rain drummed softly.

Safety on water, he rocked with a new theme:
And in the warmth of his mind's greenhouse bloomed
A poem nurtured like a chrysanthemum.

His forehead, a Prussian helmet, moody, domed,
Relaxed in the sun: a lyric was his lance.
To be loved by the people, he, a stranger, hummed

In the herring-store on Sunday crammed with drunks
Ballads of bawdry with a speakeasy stress.
Yet lonely they left him, 'one of the Yanks'.

The children understood. This was not madness.
How many orphans had he fathered in words
Robust and cunning, but never heartless.

He watched the harbour scouted by sea-birds:
His fate was like fish under poetry's beaks:
Words began weirdly to take off inwards.

Time that they calendar in seasons not in clocks,
In gardens dug over and houses roofed,
Was to him a see-saw of joys and shocks,

Where his body withered but his style improved.
A storm shot up, his glass cracked in a gale:
An abstract thunder of darkness deafened

The listeners he'd once given roses, now hail.
He'd burst the lyric barrier: logic ended.
Doctors were called, and he agreed to sail.

RICHARD MURPHY

The Woman of the House

IN MEMORY OF MY GRANDMOTHER

LUCY MARY ORMSBY

1873–1958

On a patrician evening in Ireland
I was born in the guest-room: she delivered me.
May I deliver her from the cold hand
Where now she lies, with a brief elegy?

It was her house where we spent holidays,
With candles to bed, and ghostly stories:
In the lake of her heart we were islands
Where the wild asses galloped in the wind.

Her mind was a vague and log-warmed yarn
Spun between sleep and acts of kindliness:
She fed our feelings as dew feeds the grass
On April nights, and our mornings were green:

And those happy days, when in spite of rain
We'd motor west where the salmon-boats tossed,
She would sketch on the pier among the pots
Waves in a sunset, or the rising moon.

Indian-meal porridge and brown soda-bread,
Boiled eggs and buttermilk, honey from gorse,
Far more than we wanted she always offered
In a heart-surfeit: she ate little herself.

Mistress of mossy acres and unpaid rent,
She crossed the walls on foot to feed the sick:
Though frugal cousins frowned on all she spent
People had faith in her healing talent.

She bandaged the wounds that poverty caused
In the house that famine labourers built,
Gave her hands to cure impossible wrong
In a useless way, and was loved for it.

Hers were the fruits of a family tree:
A china clock, the Church's calendar,
Gardeners polite, governesses plenty,
And incomes waiting to be married for.

How the feckless fun would flicker her face
Reading our future by cards at the fire,
Rings and elopements, love-letters, old lace,
A signet of jokes to seal our desire.

'It was sad about Maud, poor Maud!' she'd sigh
To think of the friend she lured and teased
Till she married the butler. 'Starved to death,
No service either by padre or priest.'

Cholera raged in the Residency:
'They kept my uncle alive on port.'
Which saved him to slaughter a few sepoys
And retire to Galway in search of sport.

The pistol that lost an ancestor's duel,
The hoof of the horse that carried him home
To be stretched on chairs in the drawing-room,
Hung by the Rangoon prints and the Crimean medal.

Lever and Lover, Somerville and Ross
Have fed the same worm as Blackstone and Gibbon,
The mildew has spotted *Clarissa's* spine
And soiled the *Despatches of Wellington*.

Beside her bed lay an old Bible that
Her Colonel Rector husband used to read,

And a new *Writers' and Artists' Year-book*
To bring a never-printed girlhood back.

The undeveloped thoughts died in her head,
But from her heart, through the people she loved,
Images spread, and intuitions lived,
More than the mere sense of what she said.

At last, her warmth made ashes of the trees
Ancestors planted, and she was removed
To hospital, to die there, certified.
Her house, but not her kindness, has found heirs.

Compulsory comforts penned her limping soul:
With all she uttered they smiled and agreed.
When she summoned the chauffeur, no one obeyed,
But a chrome hearse was ready for nightfall.

'Order the car for nine o'clock tonight!
I must get back, get back. They're expecting me.
I'll bring the spiced beef and the nuts and fruit.
Come home and I'll brew you lime-flower tea!

'The house in flames and nothing is insured!
Send for the doctor, let the horses go.
The dogs are barking again. Has the cow
Calved in the night? What is that great singed bird?

'I don't know who you are, but you've kind eyes.
My children are abroad and I'm alone.
They left me in this gaol. You all tell lies.
You're not my people. My people have gone.'

Now she's spent everything: the golden waste
Is washed away, silent her heart's hammer.
The children overseas no longer need her,
They are like aftergrass to her harvest.

People she loved were those who worked the land
Whom the land satisfied more than wisdom:
They've gone, a tractor ploughs where horses strained,
Sometimes sheep occupy their roofless room.

Through our inheritance all things have come,
The form, the means, all by our family:
The good of being alive was given through them,
We ourselves limit that legacy.

The bards in their beds once beat out ballads
Under leaky thatch listening to sea-birds,
But she in the long ascendancy of rain
Served biscuits on a tray with ginger wine.

Time can never relax like this again,
She in her phaeton looking for folk-lore,
He writing sermons in the library
Till lunch, then fishing all the afternoon.

On a wet winter evening in Ireland
I let go her hand, and we buried her
In the family earth beside her husband.
Only to think of her, now warms my mind.

Girl at the Seaside

I lean on a lighthouse rock
Where the seagowns flow,
A trawler slips from the dock
Sailing years ago.

Wine, tobacco and seamen
Cloud the green air,
A head of snakes in the rain
Talks away desire.

A sailor kisses me
Tasting of mackerel,
I analyse misery
Till mass bells peal.

I wait for clogs on the cobbles,
Dead feet at night,
Only a tempest blows
Darkness on sealight.

I've argued myself here
To the blue cliff-tops:
I'll drop through the sea-air
Till everything stops.

Connemara Marble

The cut is cooled by water
Douched where the discs revolve
To the drum of a far-off motor
Slicing the polished cliff,
While under the shapeless mountain
Marble-masons ponder
Souvenirs in the chunks of stone.

That gritty green-gashed line!
Why whorl it with charm
Into ash-trays and shamrocks,
Round towers, Celtic crosses?
Old men who wind the crane
Seem careless of the harm
Done to the quarried stone.

The marble of mackerel wanes
In sun on a hooker's deck,
But in shops this marble shines
Or swings from a girl's neck:
Why do the makers falter
And carve a weaker shape
Than a fish iced on a slab?

Droit de Seigneur

1820

In a grey rectory a clergyman was reading
Fortunate by firelight the *Connaught Journal*.
The shutters were closed, for famine was spreading
Among the people. The portrait of Cromwell,
One hand on the Bible, the other on a sword,
Had been stowed that evening under a haystack.
The air was crackling with the whips of rhetoric.

A groom was saddling his mare in the stable
While a redcoat stumbled down the loft ladder
Buttoning his tunic, followed by a girl
Who ran to the kitchen. The yard lantern
Yellowed the stirrups and the buckled leather
On the mare's girth as he combed her down.
The master was for hunting the Ribbonmen:

A secret band, swearing oaths by moonlight,
Refusing to pay tithes or rent to the landlord,
Who battered on lonely doors after midnight,
And wore round their sleeves a white riband.
He called it his duty to commit these rogues
To the jury of gentlemen at Galway Assizes.
Saving of property went with saving of souls.

So he galloped out with a few soldiers
On to the gravelled road under the lime-trees
With his father's pistol in a handsome holster.
They ambushed a wedding from the next parish.
All escaped except a young simpleton
In whose pocket they found a white bandage.
Twenty miles to Galway he was marched in chains.

In the pigeon park the heifers were grazing
Under the beech-trees. The soldiers had gone.
Behind the frown of the windows, browsing
On the price of cattle in the *Connaught Journal*,
The rector looked out on the frost and the sun.
The girl ran across the yard with a bucket.
'Tomorrow', he read, 'the boy will be executed.'

RICHARD MURPHY

*The God Who Eats Corn**

TO MY FATHER

WILLIAM LINDSAY MURPHY

1887 – 1965

In his loyal garden, like Horace's farm,
He asks his visitors to plant a tree.
The black shadow of the African msasa
Squats among the lawn's colonial company.

In honour among the watersprays that spin
Rainbows over the cool English rose-beds
Hand-weeded by a pink-soled piccanin
The Queen Mother's cypress nods in a straw hood.

The trees are labelled: a chairman of mines
Gave this copper beech, that silver oak
Was trowelled by a Governor: great names
Written on tags, Llewellin and Tredgold.

Livingstone's heir presented this wild fig
From the burnt-out forest of Africa:
On its branches by moonlight a boomslang swings.
This Cape creeper has a cold blue flower.

As a son I choose the native candelabra:
Perched on an ant-hill, after years of drought,
From its cut spines a milky sap flows:
To my father I give this tree as a tribute.

* *At the end of the nineteenth century there was no word in the language of the Matabele to describe the white man who came to settle in Central Africa, so he was called 'the god who eats corn'. My father, who was born in an Irish Rectory, retired from the British Colonial Service as Governor of the Bahamas and settled in Southern Rhodesia in 1950 on virgin land, where he established a farm and later a school for African children. The time is the last year of Federation – and the myth of 'partnership' – 1963.*

His own plane-tree, brought by a seed from Cos,
From the shade where Hippocrates swore his oath,
Wilts in the voodoo climate, while the gums
The trekkers imported have sapped the earth.

Under these trees, he believes that indaba*
Could heal the blood-feud. Bull-frogs crackle
In the lily-pond. Tolerant water
Eases the roots, and cools the racial fever.

From his green study half-door he looks out
On the young plantation of his old age:
An ibis is perched on a cone hut,
The rain-birds croak in the citrus orchard.

Boys are sharpening pangas at the wood-pile:
Trailers approach, filling barns from the field
With limp tobacco to be dried by steam.
A Union Jack droops on the school flag-pole.

On the kitchen steps, in kaffir quarters,
With rickety babies, the sewing-club meets,
Nagged by my mother with knitting patterns
Frail as a lily in her straw sun-hat.

Such tinkle of bangles, such ivory teeth
Clacking, they gossip of clothes and clinics.
A child rolls a pram-wheel over the earth,
A cat is stalking the cooped-up chickens.

He drives to the store to collect his *Times*
And letters from home, tulip-trees in flower,

* *In the old tribal society, the chieftain decided his policy after hearing advice from his counsellors in the shade of a large tree. This counsel was called the indaba. The tree could be any kind of large African tree, a mopani, a fig or, most likely, a msasa, a lovely deciduous tree of the bush.*

Road-grit on his tongue, tobacco booms
A memory, hot wind raising a dust-choked roar.

He swims before breakfast in a blue pool
Remembering Atlantic waves, a gothic half-light
Splashed on to hymn-books in a pitch-pine hall
Where his father preached. He prays at night.

At the carol service in the grading-shed
He reads the lesson, joining trade with truth.
My knees remember his coconut mats,
The mesh of our duty to improve the earth.

'To do some good for this poor Africa'
Was Livingstone's prayer, but not the Founder's dream.
Towards gold and diamonds, the Pioneer Column
Trekked at the bidding of a childless millionaire.

They came with ox-wagons, claiming a treaty,
To the king's kraal, his great indaba tree,
With charming letters from Queen Victoria:
There the chameleon swallowed the black fly.

In dusty dorps they slept with slave-girls,
On farms they divided the royal herd.
In stifling mine-shafts the disarmed warriors
Were flogged to work, their grazing-grounds wired.

So now at white homesteads, the coffee steams
On creepered verandahs. Racial partners
Do not mix in wedlock sons and daughters.
The white man rides: the black man is his horse.

Brown bare feet slide softly over the tiles
Soothing the master, scrubbing his bath,

Folding his towels, timidly with smiles
Smoothing his pillow, and wincing at his wrath.

To each black, his ten acres for millet;
To each white, his three thousand of grass.
The gospel of peace preached from the pulpit;
From the hungry fields the gospel of force.

In a paradise for white gods he grows old
Cutting rafters out of the felled wood,
Baking bricks from the clay of ant-hills:
He plants the first rose on the burnt sandveld.

Thirteen years ago his books were unpacked
In the path of mambas, where nomads' fires
Lit stone-age sketches on the walls of caves
And the sand was printed by lion spoor.

His Governor's helmet stowed in a teak chest,
He called back Homer after fifty years'
Damp decay in the West of Ireland:
He retired into the sunlight on a thousand acres.

Trapped from tribes in their idle forest
Negroes gathered to work for meal and poll-tax,
Their teeming women overcrawled by bony kids,
Calling him 'Baas', grinning, hungry, diseased.

They wove wicker-and-mud hovels to sleep in.
Tractors invaded the elephant road.
A bore-hole was sunk. Cicadas at his fly-screen
Halted and shrilled. The kudu retreated.

He fed corn to his gang and cured fever.
Cigarettes sold in a London shop

Kept people stooped on his kopje alive.
Each year he felled more trees to plant a crop.

Between the auction floors and seed-bed sowing
First in a thatched hut he began a school.
The market rose and fell, drought followed flooding,
When the leaves ripened there were showers of hail.

Daily at dawn, they clang the plough-disc gong
That winds a chain of men through vleis and veld.
No boss-boy drives them with a sjambok's thong.
At dusk they come to class-rooms to be schooled.

Children are chanting hymns, their lean bodies
Tropically sensual behind puritan desks,
From mealie plot and swamps of tsetse flies
Lured by the witchcraft of the god's mechanics.

A red-hot poker flowers in the playground,
A viper sleeps on the sand. The dry slate
Under the sweating palm is rubbed and scrawled.
They wait like logs, ready for fire and wind.

Tall in his garden, shaded and brick-walled,
He upholds the manners of a lost empire.
Time has confused dead honour with dead guilt
But lets a sunbird sip at a gold creeper.

His scholar's head, disguised in a bush hat,
Spectacled eyes, that watch the weaver's nest
Woven, have helped a high dam to be built
Where once the Zambesi was worshipped and wasted.

Sometimes he dreams of a rogue elephant
That smashed the discharged rifle in his hand:

Or reading, remembers the horns of buffalo,
The leopards he shipped to the Dublin zoo.

On the game-cleared plateau the settlers say
'This is our home: this is white man's country'.
Dust-storms gather to hide their traces
Under boulders balanced in a smouldering sky.

The shout for 'Boy!' from the dinner table
Long after their exodus will be recalled:
The black male hanged for a white woman's 'rape',
For loving a Negro, the fair girl gaoled.

The mission's wafer, the witchdoctor's goat,
The scoutmaster's pride in his multiracial troop,
The tobacco leaf, the whisky and soda
In the black man's bush-fire will all burn up.

Violence of love deprived of communion
Begins to bud like trees before the rains.
The safari is over: the earth needs planting
But the planters are hunting each others' skins.

Behind the msasa the Southern Cross hangs
And tom-toms hammer and the tree drum booms
And a white nun screams in petrol-bomb flames:
Silence in the shanty waiting for machine-guns.

They say, when the god goes, the rain falls,
Contour ridges burst, sweeping off crops,
The rafters crumble, trees shoot through floors,
And wind carves the fields into smooth dust-heaps.

The concrete cracks and the brown rivers bleed,
Cattle die of rinderpest, dogs with rabies

Bite their masters, the half-freed slaves are freed
But not into a garden that anyone remembers.

Now the old mopani forest is felled.
The settlers cannot cling to their laagers,
Wire for a gun-boat, profit in gold-shares,
Or wave silk flags against showers of assegais.

The trees that fail are soon devoured by ants.
Sundowners bind together a white crowd:
Some preach of partners, more sneer at the Munts
Getting cheeky, lazier than ever. He's bored.

While he recalls the *Iliad* by heart
The B.S.A. police hold rifle drill.
A pyre kindles under *Pax Britannica*.
Black politicians school themselves in gaol.

At the needlework booth in the garden fête
My mother flaps for the show to succeed.
Calabash, tripod and bamboo flute
Wait for the dancers in the smoke-filled hut.

At dusk on the stoep he greets ambassadors
From Kenya and Ceylon. The silver trays
Are lit by candles cupped in the flower borders.
Husks hang on his dry indaba trees.

Last thing at night he checks the rain-gauge
Remembering his father on a rectory lawn.
Thunder is pent in the drums of the compound.
He feels too old to love the rising moon.

JON SILKIN

Astringencies

The Coldness

Where the printing-works buttress a church
And the northern river like moss
Robes herself slowly through
The cold township of York,
More slowly than usual
For a cold, northern river,
You see the citizens
Indulging stately pleasures,
Like swans. But they seem cold.
Why have they been so punished;
In what do their sins consist now?
An assertion persistent
As a gross tumour, and the sense
Of such growth haunting
The flesh of York
Is that there has been
No synagogue since eleven ninety
When eight hundred Jews
Took each other's lives
To escape christian death
By christian hand; and the last
Took his own. The event
Has the frigid persistence of a growth
In the flesh. It is a fact
No other fact can be added to
Save that it was Easter, the time
When the dead christian God
Rose again. It is in this,
Perhaps, they are haunted; for the cold
Blood of victims is colder,
More staining, more corrosive

On the soul, than the blood of martyrs.
What consciousness is there of the cold
Heart, with its spaces?
For nothing penetrates
More than admitted absence.
The heart in warmth, even, cannot
Close its gaps. Absence of Jews
Through hatred, or indifference,
A gap they slip through, a conscience
That corrodes more deeply since it is
Forgotten – this deadens York.
Where are the stone-masons, the builders
Skilled in glass, strong first in wood;
Taut, flaxen plumbers with lengths of pipe,
Steel rules coiled in their palms;
The printers; canopy-makers –
Makers in the institution of marriage?
Their absence is endless, a socket
Where the jaw is protected neither
Through its tolerance for tooth,
Nor for blood. Either there is pain or no pain.
If they could feel; were there one
Among them with this kind
Of sensitivity that
Could touch the dignity,
Masonry of the cold
Northern face that falls
As you touch it, there might
Be some moving to
A northern expurgation.
All Europe is touched
With some of frigid York,
As York is now by Europe.

Defence

(FOR ANN)

What 'one-in-five' can do
No man can quite do

She arrived late, with this motto:
'Time used in reconnaissance
Is not time lost'. Useful hint
On how efficient our defences
Would be. Sent from the *Home Office*
On 'Work of some importance'.
And 'The first thing' she said
'Is that there will be four minutes
Of preparation before
The thing is dropped. You should
Instruct persons to stand
In the centre of what room
They like – for the blast,
Unlike the bombs of the previous war,
Will draw the walls out.
There will be no crushing
Of flesh. Instead
On all sides walls will reveal
The citizen unharmed.' Here a question,
But 'No' she said 'we have
From our *Intelligence*
Absolute assurance
Our capital is not targeted.'
Total warfare, by arrangement.
And she was sure, when pressed.
'But there will be devastation
As we now suspect, in radius
Of forty-four miles.

The water will be infected;
The light from the thing, astonishing;
Which though surprised by, we should
Not look at; but shelter
Behind some object "to reduce
Damage to the tissue"
From radiation; or shelter
Under brown paper;
Or, if you can, –
Sheets soaked in urine.'

So women who crochet, stop that;
Men labouring whose issue is
The two-handed house, set that aside.
Girls big and delicate
With child, turn on your side;
You will melt. The ravelling spider
And the scorpion whose prongs itch
Will fuse in a viscoid
Tar, black as a huge fly.
The whole of nature
Is a preying upon.
Let man, whose mind is large,
Legislate for
All passionate things,
All sensate things: the sensuous
Grass whose speech is all
In its sharp, bending blade.
Leave not a leaf, a stone
That rested on the dead
To its own dissolution.

She left then,
As if she were with her feet

Turning an enormous,
If man-made, pearl
As means of locomotion.

Meetings

I walked from the town in
Mid morning, by path that
Pierced the exhaustion of wheat.
Stone and glass lowered beneath
What I climbed. Its blue haze
Gave out, and the path sharply
Cut into blackish earth. Trees began,
Raising branches, their leaves touched
With stiffness, hale though.
One with thicker leaf and trunk
Grew separately. I could not
See men at the back.
Another, I had not seen,
Turned through the gate before
Me, moving the iron through
Its railed arc, and he left
His hand clasped over the top
Bar as he moved it on.
 It was not gentleness,
Not age, entirely.
And after he was through
He pushed the quartered metal
Back on its arc, which shook.
 I might have stopped, a pause
Of courtesy for age
But did not. As I neared him
He seemed to have forced his
Stooped walk to my side quicker
Than I to his.
 'This is the way into
The town.' 'Yes' I answered,
Forced to say what he knew.

The question seem to shake
His flesh; as if the voice
Of intellect were firm
Even in shrunk frame. He smiled slightly.
As if the thought of his
Expended shape contracted
Mine in his. I asked
If he had eaten. 'Yes'
He said, and crossed over
His hands across his stomach, hardening
His curved shape. Some earned
Hoard of thought nourished him.
'Across that field my strength dwindled.
I took from the earth my frame's
Energy. I worked it.
It took me.' I noticed then
His eyelids were too small
To cover the stiffened muscular
Sight. And as I saw,
He came close to me and,
Lifting his face to mine,
Elaborately spat onto
My mouth a thin milkiness.
I would have hit him.
Some self-tenderness
In his words, prevented me.
He slowly moved on top of
Grass trodden into earth.
From that tree he passed
I heard a core of voices
Casually bent
On profitless violence.

A Daisy

Look unoriginal
Being numerous. They ask for attention
With that gradated yellow swelling
Of oily stamens. Petals focus them:
The eye-lashes grow wide.
Why should not one bring these to a funeral?
And at night, like children,
Without anxiety, their consciousness
Shut with white petals.

Blithe, individual.

The unwearying, small sunflower
Fills the grass
With versions of one eye.
A strength in the full look
Candid, solid, glad.
Domestic as milk.

In multitudes, wait,
Each, to be looked at, spoken to.
They do not wither;
Their going, a pressure
Of elate sympathy
Released from you.
Rich up to the last interval
With minute tubes of oil, pollen;
Utterly without scent, for the eye,
For the eye, simply. For the mind
And its invisible organ,
That feeling thing.

The Violet

The lobed petals receive
Each other's nestling shape.

We share the sun's beneficence:
Frost, men, snowdrops.
Then the violet unfolds. Not an uncasing
Of the corolla, each petal compliant
To the purpose of survival, obedient to that; but as it feels
The sun's heat, that puberty
Pushes out from its earlier self-clasping
Two distinct, clenched halves. Stiffens them.
These fluttering portions that made
The bud, separately elect
To be the flower; the violet
Halves itself, pushing apart
In two separate forces;
It divides up itself, it becomes two violet portions.
It is not a conformation of members,
Each petal a tooth, an eyelash.
On the other hand, the violet is torn apart.
Its increase is by dividing;
Its stiffened petals push further apart.
It adheres to its nature; it has no maturity,
Other than this.
It requires courage, and finds that
In this unclasping of its self-worship: two palms tentatively
Open. Going both ways,
They absorb a huge circle
Of violeted air, an intent
Movement of embrace;
Created, exposed, powerful.
The air is coloured somewhat violet.
It costs itself much.

Moss

'Patents' will burn it out; it would lie there
Turning white. It shelters on the soil; quilts it.
So persons lie over it; but look closely:
The thick, short green threads quiver like an animal
As a fungoid quivers between that and vegetable:
A mushroom's flesh with the texture and consistency of a
  kidney.
Moss is soft as a pouch.

There are too many shoots though, boxed compacted,
Yet nestling together,
Softly luminous.
They squirm minutely. The less compact kind
Has struggling white flowers; closed,
Like a minute bell's clapper;
So minute that opened then, its stretch seems wide.
The first grows in damper places.
With what does it propagate?
Quiet, of course, it adheres to
The cracks of waste-pipes, velvets,
Velours them; an enriching
Unnatural ruff swathing the urban 'manifestation':
The urban nature is basemented, semi-dark;
It musts, it is alone.

Here moss cools; it has no children;
It amplifies itself.
Could that over-knit fiction of stubbed threads reproduce
Defined creatures?
It hovers tentatively between one life and another,
Being the closed-road of plants,
Its mule; spreads only its kind –

A soft stone. It is not mad.
Reared on the creeping dankness of the earth
It overspreads, smears, begrudges something
Though it is passive; spreads wildly.
It is immune to nothing;
You cannot speak of misery to it.

Death of a Son

(WHO DIED IN A MENTAL HOSPITAL AGED ONE)

Something has ceased to come along with me.
Something like a person: something very like one.
And there was no nobility in it
Or anything like that.

Something was there like a one year
Old house, dumb as stone. While the near buildings
Sang like birds and laughed
Understanding the pact

They were to have with silence. But he
Neither sang nor laughed. He did not bless silence
Like bread, with words.
He did not forsake silence.

But rather, like a house in mourning
Kept the eye turned in to watch the silence while
The other houses like birds
Sang around him.

And the breathing silence neither
Moved nor was still.

I have seen stones: I have seen brick
But this house was made up of neither bricks nor stone
But a house of flesh and blood
With flesh of stone

And bricks for blood. A house
Of stones and blood in breathing silence with the other
Birds singing crazy on its chimneys.
But this was silence,

This was something else, this was
Hearing and speaking though he was a house drawn

Into silence, this was
Something religious in his silence,

Something shining in his quiet,
This was different, this was altogether something else:
Though he never spoke, this
Was something to do with death.

And then slowly the eye stopped looking
Inward. The silence rose and became still.
The look turned to the outer place and stopped,
With the birds still shrilling around him.
And as if he could speak

He turned over on his side with his one year
Red as a wound
He turned over as if he could be sorry for this
And out of his eyes two great tears rolled, like stones, and
he died.

The Child

Something that can be heard
Is a grasping of soft fingers
Behind that door.
Oh come in, please come in,
And be seated.

It was hard to be sure,
Because for some time a creature
Had bitten at the wood.
But this was something else; a pure noise
Humanly shaped

That gently insists on
Being present. I am sure you are.
Look: the pots over the fire
On a shelf, just put;
So, and no other way,

Are as you have seen them; and you,
Being visible, make them no different.
No man nor thing shall take
Your place from you; so little,
You would think, to ask for.

I have not denied; you know that.
Do you? Do you see
How you are guttered
At a breath, a flicker from me?
Burn more then.

Move this way with me,
Over the stone. Here are
Your father's utensils on
The kitchen wall; cling
As I lead you.

It seems you have come without speech
And flesh. If it be love
That moves with smallness through
These rooms, speak to me,
As you move.

You have not come with
Me, but burn on the stone.

If I could pick you up
If I could lift you;
Can a thing be weightless?
I have seen, when I did lift you

How your flesh was casually
Pressed in. You have come
Without bone, or blood.
Is that to be preferred?
A flesh without

Sinew, a bone that has
No hardness, and will not snap.
Hair with no spring; without
Juices, touching, or speech.
What are you?

Or rather, show me, since
You cannot speak, that you are real;
A proper effusion of air,
Not that I doubt, blown by a breath
Into my child;

As if you might grow on that vapour
To thought, or natural movement
That expresses, 'I know where I am.'
Yet that you are here,
I feel.

Though you are different.
The brain being touched lightly,
It was gone. Yet since you live,
As if you were not born,
Strangeness of strangeness, speak.

Or rather, touch my breath
With your breath, steadily
And breathe yourself into me.

The soft huge pulsing comes
And passes through my flesh
Out of my hearing.

A Death to Us

A tiny fly fell down on my page
Shivered, lay down, and died on my page.

I threw his body onto the floor
That had laid its frail life next to mine.

His death then became an intrusion on
My action; he claimed himself as my victim.

His speck of body accused me there
Without an action, of his small brown death.

And I think now as I barely perceive him
That his purpose became in dying, a demand

For a murderer of his casual body.
So I must give his life a meaning

So I must carry his death about me
Like a large fly, like a large frail purpose.

Caring for Animals

I ask sometimes why these small animals
With bitter eyes, why we should care for them.

I question the sky, the serene blue water,
But it cannot say. It gives no answer.

And no answer releases in my head
A procession of grey shades patched and whimpering,

Dogs with clipped ears, wheezing cart horses
A fly without shadow and without thought.

Is it with these menaces to our vision
With this procession led by a man carrying wood

We must be concerned? The holy land, the rearing
Green island should be kindlier than this.

Yet the animals, our ghosts, need tending to.
Take in the whipped cat and the blinded owl;

Take up the man-trapped squirrel upon your shoulder.
Attend to the unnecessary beasts.

From growing mercy and a moderate love
Great love for the human animal occurs.

And your love grows. Your great love grows and grows.

Respectabilities

Many liberals don't just
Make love, they first ask each other;
And either is free to decline
What the other wishes;
That is, unmitigated
Possession of the beloved's flesh.
Nothing hasty, nothing unconsidered
Catches the liberal by
The hairs of lust. Nothing.
And this consideration
For those feelings
Of the approached one naked
In love, or in hunger
Is extended to all.
He will, for instance, ask
A starving man if he
Would eat, pressing
For the particulars
Of hunger. And inquire
Why he is deficient
In bread. All men are treated
With such perception as stones
Get in subjection to
Their shaper, as their use fits
To his. Men are chosen to meet
That judged compassion which
A liberal has. A wounded man
Receives the ointments of love
From matrons, with respect.
Sex, the inhuman hunger,
Demands courteous
Submission, polite domination.

In fact, the turning world
A stone delicately
Veined with acceptable
Colours, deficient just because
Another stone has gouged
A bit from its flesh
Demands the liberal heart;
Though a different stone
Brutal in the untamed
Components – a misshapen
Tongue of useless rock –
Merits, and gets,
A frank dismissal.
And this, too, is fair;
Though more than half the earth
Is denied purchase on
That delicate conscience
Cash gives: a fair if privileged
Mind veined with gold.

The Centre

My ancestors made love
In the hot pastures of the near east
And got me my seed there.
I should be drawn to
The Mediterranean.
I suppose I am. Greece
Was the shudder of the bird from the high hills.
But Italy; those with gold teeth
Are plucked of these by the Italian;
His main industry is fools.
His landscape gathers on the surface,
Not deepening into
The scents of heat, that delicate
Strength which breaks through
The white, Greek rock
In veins of darkness
That smell of the mineral
Origins of men.
So there is Greece. But my mind stays
In a place I saw little of.
The river drifts through
The town, falling massively
Under a low bridge.
Geneva. Was it fixed
I should choose your cool streets
Hinted of by the south?
Round this place move
The ornate schisms, intertwined
And made fast by the vicious and costly
Emblem of puissant Europe.
Is it strong only? It is also
Absurd. It is a continent

Caught in its intellect
At which centre it drops
Into a great lake;
Like some bath with its plug out.
And it is here I am
Constrained by having both
Prevailing intensities
As locked, and as formed
As the coolness is formed here
In precision from the clash
Of oppositions. Such firmness
Seems pre-determined
And intertwined to a gap
That is the weave and the space
Made by Europe in struggle,
Where choice flickers, but does not choose.
It is where the tensions meet
And wear each other away.
The life of a great
Intelligent continent
Falls through the space
It has made in itself
With too much intellect.
Or was it the intellect
Sought for a bride
But found only itself
Sufficient for its appetites, –
Say a poison this chemist
Fatally delivered
And tasted, and decayed on.

JON SILKIN

Dedication

TO MY FRIENDS

It does not matter she never knew
Who Pater was. What is rare
Despite the encirclements of marriage
Or even the political relationships
Affianced beyond parliament
Is love, which breaks the breads.
The staff of women, the dread,
The hunger of men, it is not
Just what I am capable of
If mature; it is the force
Behind those intimations of our senses
Progenitor to more growth,
If anything is. Remember,
The moulds of rock perish,
The flower so delicately formed
The minute exactness seems meant
To last. What does live
In the complex fabrics of air,
Uncoloured, and always nubile,
Is this man-like attribute.
So very carefully
Consider what you do
As an action related always
To this eternal motion
In man's leathery breast;
For the way we treat each other
In private is minutely
The way we deal with wives
And they their men. Even stones
Wrinkled in a contempt
Of their manipulators

Lie in some comradeship,
For their sakes. And for Man,
Men matter, whether that God
Who made us, and the stones,
Is watching us, or bored
With human agony
Lies in immortal sleep
Terribly locked, not witnessing
The outrages of human hunger
Bearable only because
They must be, even these uptorn
Grains of love that are burned
In complex and primitive agonies
In concentration camps.

Nature with Man

The lank summer grass
As it is, bent and wailing;
A scorching wind
Scours a whole plain of it.
Dust still oppresses. Then
As if the earth received
A bruise a pool of brown
Slime erupts slowly
From among the stems. Summer mud . . .
Hot and stagnant. The grass stalks
Stand pricked without root
In the rimless mud . . . in what eye.
On some field of grey stone
A white sud of saliva,
So fine it seems a mildew,
Agonizes over the crop.

But are the humans here? Nature
Had a human head. The mouth
Turned on its long neck, biting through
Scale, sinew; and the blood
Carried through the flesh
Beyond the ends of veins
As the severed head
Rolled into the bullrushes.
This limp and useless
Going off among tall weeds
Has soured the earth, whose body
Decays and perishes.
As for the pain
That suds onto the stone;
That, simply, is pain.

How much else is there?
There is only one head.
But it has several minds
Which still give out
Great reticulations
Of ideas, nets wilful and sharp
Over it; binding it
In pride and thought that cut
The smiling face of pleasure.

'O pity, pity, pity'?
But the weedy soul is shrinking.
Nor can it see how
To join itself unto
The membered flesh. The whole of
Nature is turning slowly
Into an eye that searches
For its most developed
And treacherous creature, man.
Monstrous and huge eye:
The entire process
Of nature perverted
Into the search for him.

The Wholeness

Tiny stones
Have misery
Unforfeited though bound with
Good roots.

The continual
Sway, deeply rooted,
Of the branches of solitudes
Shares pain.

Stones in
Their large or
Minute splendours, or the olive
That recalls

Its inner
Shape, even
The hand that planted it,
Bring little

To the flesh
With that
Spirit it nurses; we have
Small contact.

This olive,
With the hand
That scooped earth for it; masts of cedars
Poised high

In thought –
This sensuousness
This getting of images
Was never

Sensuousness,
But handled, merely;
I am a man waiting his dead wife's touch.
And I wait

As though
This getting of richness,
All unctions of spiced Asia,
The animal

Oozings of
Gums, salivas
Of odours that leaves yield
To touching,

Is nothing.
Truly this seems nothing
Compared to the modest touch
Of the hand

Gently
On cheeks, places
As curved, but laid modestly.
We did not

Share in this
Touching and yielding,
This courting sensuousness
Of earth.

If then
I was content,
I should be glorious now.
I partake

Of the olive;
I plant and reap;

I have sharing in grinding of
  What I gather.

  Yet having
The harvest I
Do not possess it; it seems
  Its granary

  But not grain.
It is increase
But formally, mine as
  Stones are.

  I therefore
Distrust that past.
Many gathered seeds without issue.
  We walked

  You, the soul,
I, the flesh, speaking
As with finger-tips held up.
  And though we

  Have use
Of these, they
Are as if rented; no man's.
  And they

  Stand from
Their wholenesses;
We are two-selved
  Creatures that

  Each with
Self-violation charges
Under the strange, live sun
  Its destruction.

The tiny stone
Of creation charges
The fluid in the crude oyster that forms
The pearl. But

No precious
Creation nor wholeness
Of charged pain beautifully
Entire

Is of me; I have no commodity.

The infinite charges of the flesh
The commodities of sensuousness,
The olive, pearl, stones of creation –
In their sensuousness these tear us.

Yet the mental
Forces billow, and joy,
If it is joy, as we are torn
Quickens you to grow;

Not as
A quick seed in stone
But as you never grew, swellings
Of wheats,

And then
The billowing of
The entire meadow of curved stem.
Silent in

The stirring
Crop, the predator
Is dismayed, and takes flight.
I perceive

Your growth,
In which
Perception plant my grain.
For I

Lived before
Through flesh only,
As it were, on some infinite store
Of images;

But on these
As the eye
Cannot touch and the hand touches,
Merely.

As the seed
Struggles with
Soil to flower with assertions
Of more seed:

We rear with
The one the other an
Infinite sensuousness of wheat
In commodity.

The dying
Body in paroxysm
Turns over: we turn
Away from

An older
Disaffection. The branches
Stir above the healed lovers.
The huge halves

Of this life are one for once.

NATHANIEL TARN

Ely Cathedral

O to laze and to lie down in my soul,
to rest on the hard light of a fen morning!
But pheasants scurrying, wet tails
tucked low behind them in the steaming grass,
tough crows choking the furrows' throats,
pigeons cooing into their breast mirrors –
beaks scratching their metallic image of the earth –
disturb the fields, ruffle the sky. The farms,
hugging their acres to their walls,
spit out thin populations, cycle or tractor mounted,
towards spine-breaking tasks:
their blood's still tea and mist
in the awakening tendrils of their veins.
Delicate animals, bred for a millionaire,
in Indian file potentially the paragons of motion,
touch empty roads with froth and whips
and rainbow silks. All at this early hour
remorseless glides into the morning's grooves
and rest is out. Why! over all the Isle of Ely
even the stones, virgin or cut, still wait
an evolution into higher states; even their queen –
the dream of immemorial saints, the sleep of kings –
at anchor: yearns towards the earth's high tides;
rich: she would sell her towers for Christ's limbs
and be as free as birds thrashing the sun
when, swerving, they turn winter over with their wings.

Grief is so Much a Now

Grief is so much a now –
the hand has not moved, and will not move –
yet the hand moves as the spine scores the earth
it weighs on, as the skull fits rock sockets, the toes
recollect that this is grass, this leaf, this twig,
as the eye roams its zenith for the eagle who will cross it
preserving his kingdom against all intrusions.

Grief is so much a now – things cry, believe me,
I have heard them. I have heard their complaint
as the hand and the eye assess them in turn.
If it would seem to you that none is linked to another,
that there is no relation between any of them,
as you go about your daily business: remember
that, at certain times, they cry all together as a choir.

The things of grief, her detailed catalogues,
are a present you will never lose; they will ensure
that you can never die. Each item floats one fare!
Grief is so much a now – that you swim with or against
the tide, no matter – as you open your mouth to cry too,
the waters that move backwards and forwards in you,
each wave of these waters you are proposes her name.

The Moon in Nō

As when the moon hides behind clouds and sulks,
waiting for the world to warm, that she might,
by contrast, hold the sky in her cool hands,
so the principal actor – *shite* – refrains
and the flute goes on and on wailing and on
until the house steams and he says: 'Now,
I am going in.' He enters with imperial sloth
as the moon passes from clouds and snows
upon the hushing mountains, at the pace of frost
to glide down glaciers – those white feet
sliding so slowly forward, the toes uplifting,
then down again to slide and slide and slide.

And when, after a man's full age of silence,
next: preparation of belly yowls and mewling,
he has talked himself and the public
into his petrified white cold,
pouring his poetry upon our heads
like a fall of silver foil, a floe of ice,
he, hidden once again, from his frail bower
helped up by all, presented, now outshines –
that perfect face so lovely one could scream
as thick male hands deliver up the voice –
he seems the sun his ghost who clasped the moon
and trembled at her cold and so divorced,

sounds in the deaf, makes even silence sigh.

Ranger Spacecraft

Where the report says it stops and 'parks'
after the first whoosh which scalds Canaveral
and hoists the whole of Florida, America even, above
that ink sea seared with orange the big jets bask on
into a fire we can no more imagine – there,
where it shifts on its axis, shoots out antennae,
shivers the cold off its flanks, appears to think,
appears to meditate on the earth's commandments,
where it still seems to belong to us, has not left us
entirely, is where I cannot help thinking of it
as of a creature outbound in heart-breaking loneliness.
When geese set out on their rapt orbits round the sky
or schools of whales furrow the aching sea,
they seem alone to us, yet have their company:
none is so lonely as that human star. That it is of man,
shine of his brain, of his fine hands finished,
that it bears such questions with it, such probes,
that it makes us turn from our hearts to what we know
and causes us to learn that we do not know, is compassion.
Take the lobster from its cave as it measures with claws
the enveloping squid and lacks salvation's span
and knows its carapace will not save it, but knows how?
Take the slush of a houseless crab on the shark's tooth,
the rabbit mumbling at the rattler's open jaw,
the fledgeling skewered on the eagle's talon –
take all that faces dying and may still ask questions.
How do they know? How do their limbs contract?
How do they gaze out, their thoughts move at the end?

For the Death of Anton Webern Particularly

Sunday gardening, hoeing, trying to think of nothing but
hoeing – so that this at least can be an exercise in the true
sense –
nevertheless I can think of little but the death of Anton
Webern.
I just happened to read it. It just happened to be Webern.
One has ferreted out and written up at length how the
Weberns
went out to dine some night with their daughter and their
(unbeknown to them) blackmarketeer of a son-in-law,
shortly
after the American occupation. The G.I. agent provocateur
went out
to block any escape. Just at that moment, in the black back
yard,
the fragile Webern, out to puff a gift cigar, collided
with the decoy who shot him by mistake. Back home, not
knowing
whom he'd killed, but withered by it, this kind man died of
drink.

Sunday gardening, hoeing, I turn over the worms in their
beds
and am shadowed by the blackbirds. And I have to ask
again from what
body-stitching those worms are sundered and picked out
writhing to die,
and from what soul-harrowing that Rome of blackbirds
flutters down
to drill and gut the worms with javelin beaks, and in the
fold of what

wedding of body and desire in Jerusalem I am conceived
and born
to offer this show. I need to ask on what Sunday God first
churned
his cauldron world in such a manner that we all deal death,
not knowing that we deal it, scarcely caring, yet dying of it
too
from afar – in what stew God first mixed meat of worm,
feather and beak of bird and hand of man and what bubbles
send up each in turn to do the other in. And how, at last,
the notes
composed by fragile Webern survive the boil and music in
the bubbles.

The Eden Foxes

'And will you believe it? Seven foxes, seven!
on the lawn!' Said I: 'There will be lions (laughing)
and tigers and perhaps elephants next!' But thrilled
and thought to myself of the wild would be there first –
before the destroyers came in our guise or another.
And indeed, yes, a perturbed slant to the tulips and lilac,
must-drift, a stench in whiffs as of weed rot far off
and cold dinners: a gashed fish here, here a black bone:
'To the butchers and fishmongers they go; they are
everywhere now the rabbits are thinning of myxomatosis.'
Across the lawn, by the garden hut Eve played in
as a child, the savaged leavings of a hen, and as she passed
holding her child, a growl and coughs beneath it.
And I pass too but get not even a growl. Yet heaven's
Wind, as once He transposed Eden, kindles, though I cannot
find: the lawn is rusted with foxes, rufous with brush
and snap-jowl. To my mind the day streams with foxes like
fire. Who have drawn Eden there, salvaged, reaped again
down to the autumn grasses Eden in splendour – O that day
of scythes as He the Lord got tired of His rest and loosed
the Eden foxes! 'They, not the snake!' . . . 'There! there!'

The Wedding

The company of those I had flown all my life
surrounded me again as if I had homed to them,
migrated back on well-worn routes. Do we know
which of his haunts a bird prefers? A secretary-
bird, haughty with parrots, a snake-crusher,
grey in the coloured riot, I await the bride.
Who came, lilting like a paradise, all of white
haloed, preening a little, so proud in her
slow sailing up that aisle as in some eastern
garden she knew best. And was suddenly by me,
I terrified by her white arrival on my grey bough.
We sang not but were sung through the black
bobbing – crows: bowing and bobbing, hissing
their psalms over us, we: passive on our boughs.
Leant over and were pecked and bibbed by crossed
parental wings as if to imprint and perpetuate
our 'instinct' for the nest. And then a glass,
like a snake's eye, in a tray below. Trained,
I shivered it with the thud of a talon,
nearly destroyed the nest it seemed to me
in the silence, and cried out a loud sentence
meaning: I take you fowl of Jerusalem to wife.
And all that day, and that night, I sang them,
whose calls or territories I owned not, and to them,
before the break, was like a balm, a flowing
like the seas between their homes – in a trance
sang them in for the last time to my bough,
filled their mouths with morning praises of me simply.

Nomad

I shall square the circle: uproot each sentiment,
hack out my heart from its beating place,
rather than be a son to righteousness.
And that is all the tending I will do, the tilling and
ploughing.
He was righteous. This is granted. Please accept it.
I mean his grid maps were correct; he had it all parcelled
out:
he knew just where each channel should flow and at what
hour,
also the rotation of crops for the best aggregate yield.
Cases were brought to him for trial. He was his own lawyer.
He would even know that so and so's son should raise such
a crop,
another be raised . . . taught this or that trade. He even cared
something for the earth.

But I want the lovely earth to flower and my cattle to graze
and laze along in a frieze along the sky just as they are.

The heart's quintessence, let me tell you, is not of
righteousness:
love is not written down with paper and ink –
not drained like that.
Your harvests in the end leaned all one way.
Everything round him wilted as in too hot a sun.

I too am woven of pity and mercy but will not yield up this
sword.

I am to forget his appalling courage and forgo all his results:
if not I wilt, if not I die too, my pastures, my cattle too.

Master Spy

They stay at home most days washing white gloves,
sheening top hats, freshening up ribbons,
polishing boots, belts, wallets.
Their uniforms are always to hand.
You can spot them, on outings, a mile off.

I wear rags like the heart.

They have people in to clean their drains, ram free
potsherds, builders' cement, the coal of snow.
Their drains are rubbed almost transparent.
You can see codes, messages, declarations,
whispers, running through them as in a stream.
From the next house, my ear sucking the wall,
I hear and know that tongue of theirs forever –
I spoke it once, took my ease in it, my comfort,
when the whole world could speak it with lions and lambs.

It stutters vexed now like blood to the heart.

Listen. Swallow to free your ears. Try to hear me.
We shall meet again very soon and converse once more.
I shall be able to translate the entire language for you.
You will grasp the tenor of whole phrases, even paragraphs.
I shall make clear to you the meaning of this war.

Your heart will start ticking over very gently again.

Last of the Chiefs

I speak from ignorance.
Who once learned much, but speaks from ignorance now.
Who trembled once with the load of such knowledge,
trembled and cried and gritted his teeth and gripped
with his fists the ends of the arms of his throne.

Who once distilled this island in his green intestines
like the whale distils her dung gone dry called ambergris –
a perfume for faraway races

who wrecked us.

Only here and there, like lightning before the rain's whips,
like a trench along the deep, a thought much as I had:

in the belly of the whale there is room for such an island.

I laugh. I come now. I clear space. My name, my very being
is that: I clear space. I pass over them with my thongs,
        laughing,
that have died fighting the island-bellied whale, not
        prevailed,
turned at last their steels against themselves, lie in spasms,
their cheek and chest muscles like rock. I pass over them,
smoke them, whip them, revive them, send them out again.

Wise wind singer with a forked tail like white lightning
and your black pin eye. Paradise tern on her tail-long hair.

I am thankful. I accept. I take your offerings of pork lard
and the myriad flowers of the scissored palm leaf. I take.
I accept. But above all I thank you for the breasts in heaven
of my daughters of the island which is Nukahiva of the
        Marquesas

that you know as Herman Melville's green garden, his
Pacific.

Some say he beautified this green back yard.
I speak from ignorance. I remember little.

The Cure

Among the rugosas and the wild, hip-loaded, feather-leaved,
thorn-warning ones it happened, not in the law-abiding
beds.
Hip-orange and white the damned thing streaked, with a
grey wash
in its mouth, and I knew, spat Oh God no and ran to the
patch.
The whole bird racket in there had maelstromed and
swirled out –
all that came back, jilted, as if drawn with stump paddles,
was a float that had not yet stained air with the softest of
greys.
Had never begun. Seemed to be swimming, discovering,
looking about.
With an idiot's sloth. The beak opening, closing, without
a sound.
Saving was out because of that red bared spine and the
thickening syrup
at the beak. Now I shall not kill a fly the size of a pinhead,
no.
My hand could not find its way through the thorns and cat
claws.
My feet came down on the early wings; they swam still,
swam still.
A big fly lashed on to the gash and held tight. I stamped
again to dye the ground. The whole bird universe with its
one
soul shuddered and winced, I know that: wings withered
in my head.
What horror-struck, astonished wrath like mine, when I
am gashed,
will hammer down its terrible extremities to comfort me?

Bring a Child Flowers

Bring a child flowers: pluck them from the air,
cut them in gardens, buy them at corner stalls,
smart shops – all one. Her smile is of one price.

If you can explain to me how it comes about
that one can adore so and wish to cripple so
in one same moment one's own life's fingers,
one's mornings' reapers, the weavers of one's nights –
I think some other poet said: I love, and hate
and I am miserable without understanding of this human
    state –
tell me with this one smile how it can be.

When I can still my nerve to her pace,
she is such gold, such reward,
not shrill at all.

The border of heaven and hell this very moment
(though I'm full of good will to bursting) reels on a nerve
which falls like a rod straight through my guts.
We do not go from health into disease
and back again to health. We crawl like animals,
nursing the worms will eat them later on,
from pain to pain. And pain's nerve runs here:

a frontier on which love and rage confuse their documents,
a no man's land in which the pass of love
meanders like my child from smiles to tears.

Do tell my children please, in black on white,
that once, when I was young and close to them,
I loved them as a god must love his fantasies
and laid my hands upon them while they slept,
willing my love to fashion in those hands

such rainbow sprays of covenanted time
as reached one season when, flower-like, they wilted

into the men and women who do not know me.

The Delivery

On her bed the sea breaks in with a Sinai sound
we are deaf to. She thinks herself a ship, tempest-split,
spreadeagled on the waves. Sailors
in gumboots and oilcloths work in silence
to save her wreck and bring her into port.
She gapes at all her sides and the sea sings in,
wallows within to wash her bulkheads clean,
to bring her prize to the surface, her dead tongues
to our ears. In there are singing's keel
and each sprung stave of her own seed's suspension,
but here, but on the bed, it is all tide, all tossing,
all wave and surf and scum – the black rubber
of harbours, the rudders' plash and suck
and gulls guzzling under skull caps of oil.

Love's mount gapes dark and is torn apart,
Jerusalem laughs through all her open doors;
he comes in a rush of dirt and slime, the prince,
slithering like a fish in the gullies of Hebron;
his hair is a black web on my altar table,
night traps her stars in snares above Gethsemane;
his eyes glare out, his head swivels,
he is preening new wings now as he waits by Jordan;
the cord is cut as he bellows his orders,
the sky's trunk, his spear, he grabs from Enoch;
blue with the world's cold, brown with its ordures,
he looks about him, counting Judah's fee;
the star of David dazzles as Israel bows down
in Babylon's dust to receive her crown.

She thinks she screams but is silent really,
as the sailors press on her for her last cargo;
she thinks she creaks along her final course

as rubber hands reach in her for the anchor now.
She thinks she screams but is silent really,
like a body handled by the washer of the dead –
white on her white sails, tangled in her cordage,
she feels no backbone beaching through the sea's shoulders
while in each gap of breath abysses yawn
as round and boundless as the whale's grey hump
gashed with the furrow of her delivery.
But she is resurrected to hear him cry, the king,
and press him to her eyes where the sea still swells,
while on her thighs the spume goes the colour of earth.

Noah on Ararat Again

FOR KIT SMART: HIS SPIRIT, HIS BEASTS IN 'JUBILATE AGNO'

Gardens on Ararat? All's green on Ararat
fading to gold as sleep lays down the year,
powdering to ash as fire melts this sleep,
as here we garden, sweeping up the leaves.

Can we blame the rose for being the most beautiful thing
in the world
or the Jew if he rot?
God how the autumn goes, how fast it goes,
in petal wine poured on the dry brown leaves.
This is a Jewish century you lot,
this compost is of falcon noses and shark lips.
I pried open young lips last night with a tongue
as sharp and darting as the hoe's in this new bed.
These are for the pot:

In my bones, in the marrow of my bones,
the humpback rusts the sea with one last thrash,
the tiger brings down whole forests in his fractured stripes,
the elephant collapses like a skyful of clouds,
the buck stutters along the ground when hit, an aimless
prayer.
Deserts burn out a snake some ninety million years:
his bones like ours are sheathed in Ararat.
My daughter's water, my son is fire,
we are all one man.

My daughter in green like the sea, in blue like the undersea,
lays down her hair in a crocus pool as the sun did on the
flood;
in her head all the earth's brains spin like spring squirrels.

This is Israel's garden.
Fruit of my prying, your bucking and God's fastening,
this seed in your brown leaves my autumn love:
here must Israel harden.
The second, a boy, on Elijah's throne, can't hold his hoe,
yet is Israel's pardon.

In my bones, in the marrow of my bones,
the prophet in his sulphurous vein raves the old world
        along.
The people wake to themselves, rise from the dung,
from the sewage and guano and fish-bones and ashes
on a pyre as high as the flood ever rose.
The Lord builds His pulse into the creeping things of the
        deep,
climbs into trees with them and settles them on earth;
His stroke guides birds in the air, homes them to Ararat,
at right angles to the sun.

My son laughs like an imbecile in his happiness and in mine
my son is a baby of six months with two teeth on the rack;
in his head the prayers sing without their words
to Elijah's tune.
He'll lead beasts up the ramp to this ramshackle kiln
clutching at potsherds with his feet as an old man does
when he goes to prune
roses of fire with burning baby faces
in a late Aryan June.

Sweep old and new up the path to this Ark
whose base the curling whale belts like God's arms;
I lunge in you with her twin flukes
to leave you dripping, you last of animals,
with unborn generations in your thighs
or heave you up the sky on two bull horns

as ruined Moses rammed his Father in the sky
where He was making love with Israel in His brazen sheets.
The word is hushed at last, bones take no glaze –
the horns of Moses grew you know as any cuckold's would.

Love, they've at last shouted themselves to a standstill,
asleep
with us as we turn;
they've cawed themselves to a whisper, a crackle of leaves,
with us as we burn:
my own hands at last are in the fire. As for my seed,
God will not mourn.

For we aren't very popular in this part of the world, my love,
and they won't say, when we light torches: 'You saved us,
thanks.'
It remains for us to take in these late animals,
these few tillers and potters to scrabble in our ashes.
Ararat is on fire, my bride, Ararat is on fire:
the scholars won't even find the last ivory bones.
The Lord is jealous again and His soured wine
addles in your brown loins, my love, on Ararat.

Old Savage/Young City

I

From the inner skin of my dreams,
from the womb's lining turned inside out,
where the soaring pine cone once nestled;
from the capsized backbone of my iron ship
that ploughed the rorqual, now a harpoon
thrust navel-deep into the fallow sky,
this knowledgeable heart, magic artificer,
convenes the mystery of all that I have ever known
and I find myself delighted again to belong to this world.

Streets like flexed muscles cannot knock me out:
I guess as far as power reaches, or indifference,
and then I have grown so used to sleep-walking
that sleep's no problem now.

Early I acquired the habit of looking for the eternal side of
 things,
tried to accomplish, in silence, what enthusiasts by the score
never even wished to begin. All for a smile's sake,
chivalrous above each proffered sacrifice.

Thus I cannot be frightened by these heroic tantrums,
this evangelism in the canyons of noon.
With trust in the continuity of all action
and stillness where the crowd core pulses;
frequently knowing I end a deed in its beginning,
tender in nurturing my small mistakes
in the daily quest for equilibrium between love and solitude,
I condemn them, knowing that I am ever of this life.
Delighted to belong to this world in my own autumn,
because I never take without giving in return,
never allowing a present even a flutter in my hand,

yet only reciprocating at the long long last
when the donor has forgotten what he gave –

for everything surrounding me forgets,
cities lose remembrance in their veins,
their ceremonial pattern fades,
their quick-step echoes die away,

only the shaman frolicks, mocking his own mask,
whole capitals crumbling while he counts his fingers . . .

an honest servant accused of selfishness!

II

That which achieves its little ends by little means consoles
me:
in a mausoleum details matter:

The way in which a nail mates with its wall,
a doormat yields under the feet of those who go in and out,
a door knob cools a sweating hand,

put me in touch with lives I have had difficulty in
reconciling,
open the algebraic eyes of paradise.

III

There is not enough room in the sausage factories
so they take new measures and kill pigs in the street.
We do that, now and again, inside our community houses
but only when some important day of the gods is at hand.

Here there is no sign of the gods in the streets
and every one walks by without raising his hat.

Some pale eyes blink but forget soon enough.

IV

The solitary man responds to matter
by taking it with him,
anchored to his soles and heels.
Others wallow in their freehold muck,
deprived of the whitewashing dividend of visions.

He who laughs within himself as he gazes around him,
seeing nothing but his eyes' laughter in others' eyes,
bears his own problems on his own shoulders
like a diminutive circus of birds,
without ever travelling from one city to another,
ever crossing a street,
or leaving a room to go down into the street,
(and so forth)
whiling his dusks away going home,
recalling his own sky and humming a love song.

V

A body on the morning after love is a jungle of smells,
inexplorable as a swamp, its sex closed.
A city after two or three weeks of being lived in,
accumulating its more and more exasperated skyscrapers,
becomes a terrified hermaphrodite looking for itself.
Male endures, female forgets.

VI

Darker than my loves themselves darker than white:

Some Capitol unscaled by technicians has engendered them
and dropped them on the streets
where they change in a trice to black swans.
Then positive is negative again within the camera,
the roofs close in with the grace of trees, excluding light.

Chocolate-eyed Cassandras, marvellous with hunger,
the black girls glisten as they walk away
more naked than if they were naked.

VII

The professional suburbs are peaceful.
Mr Western goes home, forgets time and space,
puts on a docile dressing-gown,
recovers his absolute self,
wires roses to his love.

Unless she phones from far away to say that, tonight,
she flatters another man, the next night weds another
and so until this time next week or the week after.

This anthropologist translates romance to ritual.
Each footnote's rare, already obsolete.

VIII

Aeons of frustrated flight,
the queen's nuptial indifference,
profit us nothing.
By betting all on building, man alone destroys.

No eschatology distracts the ravaging bee
from voyage to the sun. But man eliminates
time's architecture in the plan,
each nail, each brick, each girder in the mould.

I remain, planted everywhere, like pine needles.
I slouch, unwieldy as a fossil beast.
I am the lodestar of all faces, the slumbering animal.

IX

A raven death hovers above the river
grey with sarcophagi.

If the other world, as some myths have it, were similar to
ours
and if all the ocean liners went there together on a given day
sailing towards an identical fresh city
with legions of garish dead aboard
who would be helpless without their desks
and phones and sexy secretaries
or (talk of pleasures) without cigarettes
bitter and human by comparison with their smokers, still

somewhere before the latter end there should be pity for
them:
the air might be yielding and tender a few feet above the
water,
softer than in the whaling seas where coffins are of coral
and amber.

X

My face, when all is said and done, looks like a city too,
each wrinkle a street more or less in shadows by the watch,
shallow or deep, depending on its traffic of emotions.

Sometimes I lift my arms to the sky like skyscrapers
to join in similar lament, with ships coming and going,
and sometimes my thoughts follow surprising thoroughfares
with very few crossroads and intersections.
Then my logic tightens and shines, especially at night,
for a wind-thrashed old lady walks by me.

She is as beautiful as love.

On the day the earth achieved enlightenment –
as it is said: each blade of grass shall know itself
knowing the wind it bends to its own purpose –
on the day our people went down to the sea
and welcomed in the dead from the breakers,

feasting them for a week with nothing withheld,
before they took them back again to the shore;
on the day the living and the dead walked hand in hand,
harvesting to themselves their far-flung fathers
who had heaved with the whale in the deep
and haunted with their wings the arctic hare,
on that day I was exiled and came to this city.

She is as beautiful as love.

Can I ever forget her? Tonight, sitting here, now, together,
we could be anywhere in the world, in any season, at any
moment –
I have gathered her to my arms as the pines gather birds.
I call her mother and all her age-mates mother, as I once did,
I call her sister, daughter, lover, wife, and all, as I once
adored her,
by the same token of oblivion.

I am profoundly lonely within myself, lonely in the land's
bowels,
as lonely as a man can be . . . but this is not her business.

Cities devour her face.

The Rights of Man

'And Goodbye to you too old Rights-of-Man!'

Marble blitzed with lightning contrast,
skin's scarlet lining strung with green veins,
hard pearl in a soft oyster my finger plucks,
music in layers on the silent air,

this is how I should lie in you if lie I do,
this is how we should come together if at all,
only as Nature collates her impossibles,
as dark says to light: I drink you, I eat you, Come!

but not: I am this, so, such and such/ thus must make you
this (etc.), not: I am not really I but only I,
you see, in this relation to you . . . and all this tedium
when it has now been nightfall for so long.

You are astonished your art will not make marble whole,
cry printer's ink over the rights of man.
I tell you inside out I'll not requite. There is no
sea will welcome in this river where it flows.

Paolo's Dream

'quel giorno più non vi leggemo avante'

The amount the night must have worked
to strip away time's accretions,
to undress you to such a long ago!

When a dream
washes you young and clean
as once you were –
when gates as tall as temples,
but of metal not horn,
run apart on silent grooves, revealing you
smiling, cooking a dish perhaps you used to grant me
as a kind of token of further welcome

who left a crater in my life no meteor fills,

though almost invisible and so deep the wound's root now,
though memory says don't apologize any more
and it is not goodbye in that bath you add to with tears

but my love, my love, good morning, I'm saying over and
  over
until something there, some detail in the room, a brush,
a razor, shudders with treachery that cannot

ever heal:

legends are dying everywhere
and I can't tell how long it will take to return to you,
to meet by chance on a street corner, in the flesh,

years, maybe years . . .

My rooms close in on me, books oppress me, pens

stab me, clocks twine their hands round my nerves;
I let out a small scream to cover a big one

that would have put an end to all noise for always,

small as you were in the gap of those gates, and distant.

Baptizing Masai

They wait, once a year,
black, robed in white air.
White nuns come, once a year,
in black pumpkins of cloth.

Between them the river
nuns ford on foot.
Flamingo flights:
think of a pink leather flag

slapping a furious wind.
Not white, Lord, not black:
but striped all our endeavours
like zebra.

How themselves they are,
how themselves in experimental worlds
that spin about them huger than Africa
and empty at the nucleus.

Some are sent in veils and flounces,
dazzling pink with bouncing bosom,
bend down, décolletées,
varnish black nails with pink

to grant them our substitute angels,
love's bubble tracks.
Two nuns, ugly and old,
pray that they may be allowed to give,

not knowing yet, not at death's door,
they've given all there is.
Black dignity is that of spears.
They partition the sun.

Come closer, over the river.
The water pearls on your black heads
like oil. Come closer, a little closer.
This could be one possible world.

The Life we do not Lead

The life we do not lead
looks down on us from both these banks and laughs
as Westminster delivers us into this tossing boat;

the life we do not lead
has the sleek hulls of ships moored to each bank
strange in our need as women and just as ignorant

of what they will put down;
the life we do not lead
keeps the sharp beaks of gulls to tear with and these wings

to beat itself to puffs of smoke in time for Charing Cross;
the life we do not lead
cannot be numbered as the Tower's stones

yet we evoke it corking down the Thames,
freezing in this late Spring, pretending Summer
smells somewhere like these boats –

What do I make of this, you know, our being bound,
bound by the life we really lead and down at heel
(our boots cold fudge where slippers tripped the Globe)

in Shakespeare's year, and pitch so thin in England?
From here ships sailed that bound the mummy world,
great spiders on the wind, their sails like spider webs

and held the huge Pacific in those sails
as I hoard all the dreams the spinner heart can weave –
the life we do not lead

shrinks to a matchbox tossed on a minor sewer
as we, led by the lives that part us, abdicate,
melting into a mush for fish who've never even seen the sea.

The Stain

The stain of silence spreads
engulfing more and more of our lives,
casting shadows in almost all our rooms,
on all our stances:

It is because freedom you see has become
in this particular place a slave of silence,
because love here has no name and no tongue,
not even the memory of such instruments
and because when I wake in the morning
the night I find has devoured all my limbs,
making of me a secret I cannot afford to keep –
and limbless I cannot walk arm in arm with disaster
as a poet should.

There would have to be another beginning somewhere,
the tax of silence should be cut, our duty paid:
waking one morning crippled I would have to say
because the sun is shining for once in this dark
you give me back limbs. And you give me back voice
as if mankind were talking, and you give me back smile
as if all flowers woke together irrespective of seasons
and eyes as if the birds had grafted their bright beads on me
to grant me a side of sight.

Dawn draws white sheets like blinds over our limbs.
Last night's tide-turning I must break to tell,
break rather like the broken level of your eyes,
one higher than the other as we stammered love,

reversing floods of silence to generate new worlds.

Dispersal

I have given away the last roses.
The days are drained of light like roses
blowing too late, without the strength for colour,
dead in a crib of dry leaves.
Take it that I have made love to the sea
without a residue.

All that it needs to make the roses fade
has led us to this bed of truth
where all our dikes are breached.
Here clothes were dropped like wreaths
cast along the waves
while we gave each other our names.

Now we go back, anonymous as water,
now I resign you back to your possessions
and your possessed. Somewhere the earth is spinning
all by itself. With it we spun
one turn, locked in each other's arms,
each of us making love to one sea.

It is a lone and trackless miracle
to understand the language of your eyes
free of their glance of duty at those tides
which nudge us here. Now, love, I bless
our firstborn death, the master of this ship,
taking my way with monsters, letting you go.

Where Babylon Ends

'Nec Babylonios temptaris numeros'

Where Babylon ends
no one knows now.

I'd like before the world is ripe
to make men cry for what they are
once and for all so that
they never cry again
and this old top
stops spinning –
for then we can begin

to clarify the city,
to build with bricks you know
tall cliffs of fiery letters
far, far from Babylon
to touch the thunder's lips –
but where Babylon ends
no one knows now.

I am Hebrew they say,
i.e. I do not understand
the gambler's spinning wheel,
the rules of wanton chance,
raps on the knuckles for Jupiter's triplets,
the sag in each thread of our lives:
art for art's sake.

It may be true. It may be true.
Where they preach this, in any case:
silence. With us, a generation gone,
the ache of standstill
and then quite suddenly

the recovered gasp
of the teaching breath.

Now lights will flash on
and off in quick succession.
Flat on your bellies you will be amazed
by simple things
violently lit, then occulted.
Leave labyrinths to birds and moles
who brook no obstacles

but men wish clear well-water.
In the cracks of Babylon
willows grow
where light awakes.
I rise to the holy Jerusalem of all angels
and speak to you in those provinces
she has in every nook and cranny of your countries.